Northern Ontario Manna

Danni Peters

Copyright number 1210600

Northern Ontario Manna

Danni Peters

Northern Ontario Manna © 2024 by Danni Peters.
All rights reserved.

Published by B & F Publishing.

All rights reserved. This book contains material protected under Canadian and Federal Copyright Laws and Treaties. Any unauthorized reprint or use of this material is prohibited. No part of this book may be reproduced or transmitted in any form or by any means, electronic or mechanical, including photocopying, recording, or by any information storage and retrieval system, without express written permission from the author.

Identifiers:

Canada copyright 1219736
ISBN: 978-1-778-2441-4-8 (hardback)
Available in hardback only.

Scripture quotations are taken from the Holy Bible, New Living Translation Copyright 1996, 2004, 2015 by Tyndale House Foundation. Used by permission of Tyndale House Publishers, a Division of Tyndale House Ministries, Carol Stream, Illinois 60188

All rights reserved.

Formatting by Felicity Fox

Cover Design by: B & F Publishing

Contents

Introduction   1
Plants   3
Recipes   17

Introduction

Foraging for food can be a lot of fun and highly educational. Many areas of Northern Ontario are abundant in 'manna'. Manna was the supernatural food God gave to the Israelites during their forty years wandering through the desert.

In the gospel of John, Jesus refers to himself as the 'bread of life' and the true manna from heaven. He says, "I am the living bread that came down from heaven. If anyone eats of this bread, he will live forever. And the bread that I will give for the life of the world is my flesh." (John 6:51)

When the Israelites were in the desert, God gave them a miraculous food substance that came with the morning dew and looked like frost on the ground. Exodus 16:31 describes it as something like 'coriander seed, white, and it's taste was like wafers and honey.'

The provision of 'manna' from heaven was not just about physical sustenance. It was also a form of spiritual food, a daily reminder of Gods' constant presence and care.

It makes perfect sense that God is still supplying us with 'manna' to this day.

Living in Northern Ontario, Canada, can lead to a discovery of many types of edible plants. I have gathered information on a few of these magnificent plants and made a short compilation of what they can be used for. Many common everyday plants can be enjoyed in a variety of recipes.

Apples

There are many reasons of why apples are a healthy eating choice. Apples are high in pectin – a soluble fibre – and are packed with flavonoids such as quercetin. Flavonoids are compounds that help give the colourful pigment to fruits and vegetables and some research suggest that they assist with reducing the risk of heart disease, cancer, stroke, asthma, and type two diabetes. Apples have existed as a wild fruit since prehistoric times and have been cultivated for more than three thousand years. There are fifteen main varieties of apples that are grown in Ontario, Lake Erie, Lake Huron and Georgian Bay.

Crab Apples

Crab apple (Genus Malus) is a deciduous tree that differs from the orchard apple in bearing smaller, often acidic or astringent fruits. The fruits are valued for their jelly making properties and as preserves. Crab apples are safe to eat and though smaller in size, they contain all the healthy nutrients found in domesticated apples.

BERRIES

Blackberries

Blackberry, a usually prickly fruit-bearing bush known for its dark edible fruits. Blackberries are a fairly good source of iron, vitamin C, and antioxidants and are generally eaten fresh, in preserves, or in baked goods such as cobblers and pies. The antioxidants, vitamins, and minerals found in blackberries deliver a variety of health benefits. Antioxidants such as anthocyanins hold many anti-inflammatory and anti-microbial properties. They may also combat diabetes and certain kinds of cancer.

Blueberries

These small, round berries are about 0.2 – 0.6 inches (5-16 mm) in diameter, and their colour can range from blue to purple. Different kinds of blueberries exist, so their appearance may vary slightly. The two most common varieties are high bush and lowbush blueberries. They are also low in calories and fat. They're mainly made up of carbs and water but also contain a decent amount of fibre. Blueberries may decrease your risk of heart disease, boost brain health, lower blood sugar levels, and improve insulin sensitivity.

Raspberries

Raspberries are a small, sweet fruit, and each delicate raspberry is packed with vitamins, minerals, antioxidants, and fibre. Raspberries can be found in four different colours: red, black, purple and gold. Red raspberries are the most common. Raspberries contain much less sugar than most fruits – just five grams in an entire cup, making them less likely to raise your blood sugar levels.

Strawberries

Strawberries are very healthy, containing many antioxidants and vitamins. Usually consumed raw and fresh, these berries can also be used in a variety of jams, jellies, and desserts. Strawberries' carbs consist mainly of fibre and simple sugar. Strawberries are a good source of Vitamin C, manganese, folate (vitamin B9), and potassium. They contain small amounts of several other vitamins and minerals. Strawberries may decrease your risk of heart disease and cancer, as well help regulate blood sugar. Strawberry allergy is rather common, especially among children.

Choke Cherries

Chokecherry is found throughout Ontario and on the Canadian Shield from Quebec to Manitoba. The berries are delicious and can be used to make jelly. Chokecherry trees are a food source for many species. Large mammals such as moose and elk browse leaves and twigs. Other mammals, such as bears and rabbits, and birds eat the fruit. In most locations, chokecherry season is mid-August to early September.

Daisies

This is a great plant to add to salads and cold dishes as the entire plant can be eaten raw. The flowers have a mild taste compared to the leaves. Toss them in a salad or sprinkle them on top of a finished dish for a great, edible flower garnish.

Dandelions

People have used dandelion in form of traditional medicine for centuries. The nutritional content of dandelion extends to all parts of the plant. Dandelion is a rich source of fibre and many vitamins and minerals. People often consume dandelion leaves, stems, and flowers in their natural state. You can eat them cooked or raw. The root is usually dried, ground, and used as a tea or coffee substitute. If you eat its' greens, roots, and flowers in their whole form – in salads, baked dishes, sides and snacks – this root vegetable makes a unique, nutritious addition to your diet.

Cattail

Cattails are characterized by their small brown flowers and long blade-like leaves. Cattails reach heights of three to ten feet tall. The entire plant is edible and is a traditional food source. The tight heads are often dry inside even after a heavy rain, making this essential survival timber. Inside the stalks of fresh shoots is tasty food that can be eaten as is, sauteed, or tossed into a stir fry. The lower parts of the leaves can be used in a salad; the young stems can be eaten raw or boiled; the young flowers (cattails) can be roasted.

Clover

Clover is both edible and potentially beneficial to your health. You can eat the leaves in a salad or boil the blossoms to make tea. Clover is often used as a medicinal herb. Clover is edible by humans, although red clover should be avoided by pregnant women. The plant is a traditional

Native American food, which is eaten both raw and after drying and smoking the roots.

Black Trumpet Mushrooms

Usually found in deciduous woods, the charcoal-coloured black trumpet mushroom has a delicate structure, with gently flared and curled ends. Many people use black trumpets with fish, egg dishes, and soups. In mid-summer, typically early July through October, they can be harvested.

Chaga

Beta-D-glucans found in chaga mushrooms help balance your immune system. This means that they can stimulate your immune system when you need a boost and downregulate it when it is overactive. Chaga tea is made from the chaga mushroom, which typically grows on the trunks of birch trees in the northern hemisphere.

How to brew chaga chunks in a slow cooker/crock pot.

Step 1. Use one golf ball sized chaga chunk per gallon of water.

Step 2. Add the chaga chunks and water to crock pot.

Step 3. Set your crock pot on low and brew for 3-5 hours or until desired darkness is reached.

Step 4. Serve hot or as iced tea.

Rhubarb

Rhubarb is a spring vegetable and red stalks have a stronger, sweeter more robust flavour than green stalks, but both are fine to cook with. The stalks come into season in late March to early April and stick around until the beginning of June. Rhubarb is a vegetable often categorized as a fruit. Due to its sourness, it's regularly sugared for use in jams and desserts. Rhubarb is a good source of fibre and antioxidants. It is a popular ingredient in crumbles, pies, and jams.

Maple Blossoms

The largest maple species on the North American continent, this tree grows up to 80 feet (24m) tall. The sap and flowers are edible. The flowers in springtime are rich with nectar and can be tossed into a salad, added to baked goods or made into fritters.

Rose Hips

Rose Hips are rich in antioxidants that can help protect against cell damage from free radicals. Compared with other fruits and vegetables, rose hips offer one of the highest levels of vitamin C. This vitamin, along with other compounds in rose hip tea, help strengthen and protect your immune system. Rose hips look like miniature red or orange apples and are found just below the flower petals of roses. Fresh rose hips can be used for tea by first rinsing them well to remove any dirt and debris. Next, place four to eight rose hips in a cup of boiled water. Let the tea steep for ten to fifteen minutes and then remove the fruits. If you find the tea too tart, try adding a sweetener like honey to help balance out the flavour. Rose Hip tea can be enjoyed both freshly brewed or iced.

Fiddleheads

Fiddleheads or fiddlehead greens are the furled fronds from a fledgling fern, harvested for use as a vegetable. Available seasonally, fiddleheads are both foraged and commercially harvested in spring. The vegetable is typically steamed, boiled and sauteed before being eaten hot, with sauce, butter, lemon, vinegar and garlic. Fiddleheads can also be pickled. The cooking time recommended by health authorities is fifteen minutes if boiled and ten to twelve minutes if steamed.

Wild Mint

The leaves of raw mint are edible, raw or cooked. Having a quite strong minty flavour with a slight bitterness, they are used as a flavouring in salads or cooked foods. An herb tea can be made from the fresh or dried leaves.

Wild Rice

Wild rice, called manoomin in Ojibwe, has significant cultural importance to the Indigenous peoples of the Great lakes. It is indigenous to the Great Lakes region of North America, where it grows naturally in freshwater lakes and waterways. It is a wild grass that grows from seed annually and produces a valuable grain. Despite its name, manoomin isn't truly rice at all, but a cereal. This grain's rich, nutty character makes it the perfect pairing with savoury dishes, fresh fish or as an addition for soups and salads.

Northern Ontario Manna Recipes

TEA
CEDAR, PINE, SPRUCE

Many pines, spruces and non-poisonous conifer trees can make similar teas with strong amounts of vitamin C. Simply boil the needles/scales with water, steep until cool enough to drink, pour off any film and enjoy.

   Cedar Tea: Simmer two cups of fresh cedar in four cups of boiling water for about ten minutes until the water becomes a golden colour. Strain off the cedar and sweeten with maple syrup, to taste.

   Pine Tea: To make this tea, you will need a large handful of fresh pine needles from the tree. Cut or chop the twig and needles into one- or two-inch pieces (it should equal about 1/3 to ½ cup). Place the needles and twigs into a tea kettle or pot and cover it with about three cups of water. Bring to a boil at high heat, then reduce heat to simmer for approximately five minutes. If using a pot, cover it. After removing from the heat, you may wish to let the tea steep for five to ten minutes. Then, pour the tea through a strainer. Add honey to sweeten and enjoy.

    Spruce Tea: Add the spruce tips to the teapot and cover with boiling water. The amount of spruce tips you add will depend on how strong you like your tea. Let the spruce tips steep for ten to fifteen minutes before pouring through a tea strainer. Stir in any extra add-ons you might like, serve hot or cold.

Lilacs

Lilac Blossom Tea

Ingredients:

2 Tablespoons of lilac blossoms
250 – 300 ml boiling water
Sweetener of your choice (optional)

Instructions:

1. Pull two tablespoons of lilac blossoms off the stem.
2. Steep lilac blossoms in hot water for five minutes.
3. Remove the blossoms from the tea.
4. Add a sweetener if needed.
5. Sprinkle two to three blossoms over the tea for the typical lilac scent.

Lilac Honey

Ingredients:

Local, pure honey
Freshly picked lilac flowers
Jar size of choice (1/2-pint, pint, quart etc.)

Instructions:

1. Fill the jar with freshly picked flowers with a little room at the top.
2. Pour over honey to the top and cap.
3. Allow the honey to infuse for at least six weeks.
4. No need to strain it afterward – eat the flowers along with honey.

Dandelion Honey

Making dandelion honey is simple. All you need to do is harvest dandelion blossoms, clean the petals from the green parts, and then simmer them with water and sugar until it thickens.

Fried Dandelions

Ingredients:

2 cups of all-purpose flour
2 tablespoons of seasoned salt
1 tablespoon of black pepper
4 large eggs
80 dandelion blossoms (remove stems)
½ cup of butter

Instructions:

1. Combine flour, seasoned salt, and pepper in a mixing bowl until evenly combined; set aside.

2. Beat eggs in a mixing bowl and stir in dandelion blossoms until completely coated.
3. Melt butter in large skillet over medium heat.
4. Remove half of the dandelion from egg mixture and allow the excess egg to drip away.
5. Toss in flour until completely coated.
6. Cook coated dandelions in the melted butter until golden brown, stirring occasionally, about five minutes.
7. Drain on a paper towel-lined plate.
8. Repeat with the remaining dandelions.

Easy Rhubarb Recipe

Ingredients:

6 cups chopped fresh rhubarb
1 cup of sugar
2 tablespoons of water

Instructions:

1. In a saucepan, combine the rhubarb, sugar, and water.
2. Simmer over low-medium heat for about fifteen minutes, or until all the sugar has dissolved and the rhubarb has broken down.

Triple Berry Salad

Ingredients:

Berries: strawberries, blueberries, and blackberries
Honey

Instructions:

1. Place the berries in a large bowl and drizzle the honey over the top. Toss gently to coat.
2. Garnish with mint leaves(optional) and serve.

Maple Syrup

Maple syrup can be made from any species of maple tree. Trees that can be tapped include sugar, black, red, silver maple and box elder trees. Of all the maples, the highest concentration of sugar is found in the sap of the sugar maple.

Maple syrup is made by boiling the sap found in maple trees at a set temperature to reduce its water content. During this process, the sap thickens to the consistency of a syrup and its sugar levels increase until the distinctive flavour so many of us recognise as maple is reached.

How to make Canadian Maple Syrup.

1. First, drill a small hole in a maple tree, then insert a spout and collect the sap that drips out of the tree. The sap is mildly sweet and is mostly made up of water with a small amount of sugar.
2. Once the sap is collected you need to remove some of the water. So, simply

boil the sap in a pot on the stove. As the sap boils, the water is removed and the amount of sugar in the liquid is concentrated.
3. Once you have removed enough water and cooked the sap to a concentration of 66 – 68% sugar, you have pure maple syrup.

Daisy in Sweet Chili Sauce

Ingredients:

1 bunch of crown daisies
2 tablespoons soy sauce
4 tablespoons sweet chili sauce
1 tablespoon sesame oil
1 teaspoon sesame seeds

Instructions:

1. Put a medium saucepan of water on the stove to boil. While that heats up, wash the crown daisies and chop them roughly in half so that one half has the thick stems, while the other is thinner with the leaves.
2. In a medium bowl whisk together the soy sauce, sweet chili sauce and sesame oil.
3. Once the water has boiled, add the thick stems to the boiling water and quickly blanch for 30 – 50 seconds.
4. Remove the stems from the pot (save boiling water) and let drain in a colander. In the same boiling water add the half of

the greens with leaves and allow to blanch for 15 – 30 seconds.
5. Add the leafier parts of the greens to the colander and shock with cold water to prevent any further cooking. Gently squeeze out as much water as possible and leave to drain for a few minutes.
6. In a serving bowl toss the greens in the sweet chili sauce. Sprinkle sesame seeds on top.

Easy Sauteed Fiddlehead Recipe with Garlic

Ingredients:

2 Tablespoons olive oil
2 cloves garlic minced
½ teaspoon Chili Flakes or to taste
3 tablespoons Shallot or Scallions finely sliced
1 lb Fiddleheads approximately 3 cups washed and trimmed
½ teaspoon Salt + 2 tablespoons salt for blanching
½ teaspoon ground black pepper

Instructions:

1. Blanch fiddleheads: Bring 8 cups of water and 2 tablespoons salt to a boil. Once boiling, add washed fiddleheads and stir. Cook fiddleheads for ten minutes. Remove and plunge into ice water or rinse with cold water to cool quickly, then spread on a clean towel to dry.

2. Heat oil in a medium sauté pan on medium-low heat. Add garlic, chili flakes, shallots and salt and stir gently for one minute.
3. Increase to medium-high heat. Add in fiddleheads and sauté for 5-10 minutes stirring or tossing frequently until well heated through and a few brown spots start showing. Season with salt and pepper to taste and serve.

Sauteed Dandelion Greens

Ingredients:

2 teaspoons of salt
1-pound dandelions greens, torn into 4-inch pieces
2 tablespoons of oil
1 tablespoon of butter
½ onion thinly sliced
¼ teaspoon red pepper flakes
2 cloves garlic, minced
Salt and ground black pepper to taste
1 tablespoon grated parmesan cheese

Instructions:

1. Dissolve 1 teaspoon salt in a large bowl of cold water: add dandelion greens and allow to soak for ten minutes. Drain.
2. Bring a large pot of water with one teaspoon of salt to a boil; add greens and cook until tender, 3 – 4 minutes. Drain and rinse with cold water until chilled.

3. Heat oil and butter in a large skillet over medium heat. Add onion and red pepper flakes; cook and stir until onion is tender, about five minutes.
4. Stir in garlic and cook until fragrant, about 30 seconds more. Increase heat to medium-high and add dandelion greens. Continue to cook and stir until liquid has evaporated, 3 – 4 minutes. Season with salt and pepper.
5. Sprinkle greens with parmesan cheese to serve.

Blueberry Bannock

Ingredients:

3 cups flour
1 teaspoon of salt
2 tablespoons baking powder
1 cup of water
Vegetable oil or lard
1 cup blueberries

Instructions:

1. Mix half the flour with the remaining dry ingredients.
2. Add water until the mixture becomes thick.
3. Add more flour until the dough mixes in.
4. Heat the oil or lard over a medium-high heat until hot.
5. Break off small pieces of the dough, about ½ inch thick.
6. Place the pieces in the hot oil, turn after about 3 minutes, or when golden brown.

7. Place the Bannock on a paper towel to soak up excess grease.

Instead of blueberries, try using raspberries, blackberries and strawberries.

Maple Flower Fritters

Ingredients:

½ cup of flour
½ teaspoon baking powder
Pinch of salt and herbs and spices of choice
2 eggs beaten
¼ cup of milk
¼ cup oil for frying

Instructions:

1. In a bowl, mix flour with salt and herbs or spices
2. In another bowl, whisk eggs with milk
3. Turn a medium sized sauté pan on medium-high heat and add oil.
4. Once the oil is heated, dip maple flower clusters in the egg mixture first, then dust them with the flour mixture, and place them in the pan.
5. Place 4 – 5 in the pan at a time. When the fritters are golden brown, flip them and let them brown on the other side. Let them drain on paper towels. Serve hot.

Raspberry No-Bake Cheesecake Balls

Ingredients:

Cream cheese
Granulated sugar
Fresh Raspberries
Cool Whip whipped topping
Graham crackers crumbs

Instructions:

1. Place the cream cheese in a large mixing bowl with the sugar and whip with an electric hand mixer on medium speed until smooth.
2. Add in the raspberries and stir to combine.
3. Add in the whipped topping and fold it in. Cover with plastic wrap and place the no-bake cheesecake filling in the freezer for 2 hours.
4. Place the crumbs into a small bowl.
5. Line a sheet tray with parchment paper.

6. Scoop out dollops of the cream cheese mixture. Place the cheesecake bites, one at a time, into graham crumbs, and roll around in the crumbs until coated. (If you notice the cheesecake mixture becoming too loose to handle, put it in the freezer to set up again.)
7. Place the coated cheesecake bites onto the lined sheet tray and repeat.
8. Place sheet tray(s) in the freezer for a couple of hours until they are frozen. When ready to serve, let sit out for five minutes at room temperature.

This recipe also works for blueberries, blackberries, and strawberries.

Cattail Shoot 'Sunomono'

Ingredients:

2 teaspoons white sugar
½ teaspoon soy sauce
2 tablespoons vinegar
1.5 cups cleaned and sliced cattail shoots (white and very light green parts only)
1 tablespoon sesame seeds
1 scallion/green onion, thinly sliced

Instructions:

1. Pour sugar into a small salad bowl. Add the soy sauce and vinegar and whisk until the sugar has dissolved.
2. Add the sliced cattail shoots and sesame seeds and toss in the dressing.
3. Sprinkle with sliced scallion and serve.

Easy Apple Pie

Ingredients:

1 package pastry for a 9-inch double crust pie.
¾ cup white sugar, or more to taste
1 teaspoon ground cinnamon
6 cups thinly sliced apples
1 tablespoon butter

Instructions:

1. Preheat the oven to 450 degrees.
2. Line a 9-inch pie dish with one pastry crust: set second one aside.
3. Combine ¾ cup sugar and cinnamon in a small bowl. Add more sugar if your apples are tart.
4. Layer apple slices in the prepared pie dish, sprinkling each layer with cinnamon-sugar mixture.
5. Dot top layer with small pieces of butter. Cover with top crust.
6. Bake pie on the lowest rack of the preheated oven for 10 minutes. Reduce

oven temperature to 350 degrees and continue baking until golden brown and filling bubbles, 30 – 35 minutes more.
7. Serve warm or cold.

Berry Infused Iced Tea

Ingredients:

8 ½ cups water divided.
5 tea bags
2/3 cup of sugar
2 cups raspberries
2 cups blackberries
Juice of 1 lemon

Instructions:

1. Bring 4 cups of water to boil in a saucepan. Stir in the sugar until dissolved. Remove from heat and add the tea bags. Steep for 6 - 8 minutes. Discard tea bags.
2. In a separate saucepan add the raspberries, blackberries and ½ cup of water. Bring to a boil, then reduce heat and simmer uncovered for 3 – 5 minutes stirring and mashing occasionally. Strain the mixture into a medium heat proof bowl. Discard the pulp and seeds.

3. In a pitcher combine the tea, berry juice, juice of 1 lemon and an additional 4 cups of water. Stir, chill, and serve over ice.

Strawberry Pancakes

Ingredients:

Strawberries
Flour
Butter
Eggs
Sugar
Vanilla
Salt
Milk

Instructions:

1. Make the batter.
2. Whisk together the dry ingredients.
3. Melt the butter.
4. Whisk together the wet ingredients (melted butter, egg, vanilla, milk)
5. Add the wet ingredients to the dry ingredients, whisk them until well combined. There may be a few lumps, don't worry about these.
6. Leave the batter to rest for 10 minutes.

7. While the batter is resting, dice strawberries into 1 cm cubes.
8. Fold the diced strawberries into the pancake batter.
9. Heat a pan to medium heat. Add a little butter or oil to the surface of the pan.
10. Scoop one-quarter cup of the batter and pour it onto the heated pan.
11. Watch for small bubbles to appear on the surface of the pancake and burst, when you see them, it's time to flip the pancake.
12. Pour maple syrup over the pancakes and enjoy.

Perfect Wild Rice

Ingredients:

1 cup wild rice
At least 6 cups of water.
Optional seasonings: salt (to taste), 1 to 2 teaspoons extra-virgin olive oil, maybe 1 minced clove of garlic or 1 thinly sliced green onion.

Instructions:

1. Bring a large pot of water to boil, using at least 6 cups of water per 1 cup rice. Thoroughly rinse the rice in a fine mesh colander under running water.
2. Add the rinsed rice and continue cooking, reducing heat as necessary to maintain an active simmer, for 40 minutes to 55 minutes. It's done when the rice is pleasantly tender but still offers a light resistance. If you see any grains bursting open down the center seam, it's likely done.

3. Drain the rice and return the rice to the pot (off the heat). Stir in any seasonings you'd like to add. If you have the time, place a tea towel over the pot, cover, and let it rest for 10 minutes (this absorbs any excess moisture.) Use as desired.

Clover Salad

Ingredients:

Clover leaves and blossoms
2 teaspoons finely chopped mint
75 g (3 oz) rice
2 tablespoons olive oil
2 tablespoons freshly squeezed orange juice

Instructions:

1. Cook the rice until tender in boiling salted water, drain and mix with oil and orange juice while still hot.
2. Wash the clover leaves, split into leaflets and trim stalks.
3. Stir clover leaves and mint into the rice.
4. Split the clover blossoms into florets and use as a garnish.

Other edible plants found in Northern Ontario:

Asparagus
Black Walnut
Common Evening Primrose
Elderberry
Garlic
Hazelnut
Hickory
High Bush Cranberry
Japanese Knotweed
Jerusalem Artichoke
Lamb's Quarters
Morels
Stinging Nettle
Watercress
Wild Ginger
Wild Leek

Traditional Plants and Indigenous Peoples

Indigenous peoples in Canada collectively used over 1000 different plants for food, medicine, materials, and in cultural rituals. Many of these species remain important to Indigenous communities today. Some of these foods are like those eaten today: root and green vegetables, fruits, nuts, berries, seeds and mushrooms. Indigenous peoples also used plants as sweeteners, flavourings and beverages: many wild plants provided more than one type of food. Indigenous practitioners were skilled in the selection, preparation and dosage of herbal medicines, and traditional treatments were effective in treating a host of ailments, including wounds, skin sores, gastrointestinal disorders, coughs, colds, fevers and rheumatism. Tobacco is of major importance to many peoples, figuring prominently in ceremonies, everyday life and creation stories. Indigenous peoples use tobacco, sage, sweetgrass and cedar for various spiritual purposes in smudging ceremonies, where smoke is fanned over the face and head.

It is important to follow traditional protocol that pays respect to Mother Earth when harvesting sacred plants. Aboriginal people maintain a special connection and certain respect for the plants, trees, and roots.

Nehemiah 9:20

"You also gave Your good Spirit to instruct them, and did not withhold Your Manna from their mouth, and gave them water for their thirst."

Other Books By Danni Peters

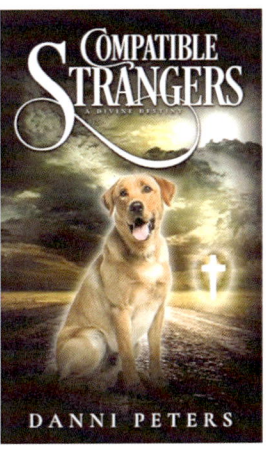

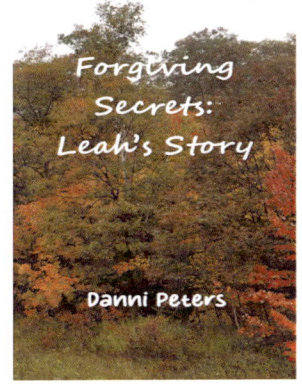

Check out Felicity's website for all your editing and publishing needs.

www.ingramcontent.com/pod-product-compliance
Lightning Source LLC
Chambersburg PA
CBRC092058200426
43209CB00067B/1866